D0913946

NILE CROCODILE VS. HIPPOPOTAMUS

BY KIERAN DOWNS

™

BELLW

TM

Torque brims with excitement
perfect for thrill-seekers of all kinds.
Discover daring survival skills, explore
uncharted worlds, and marvel at mighty
engines and extreme sports. In *Torque* books,
anything can happen. Are you ready?

This edition first published in 2022 by Bellwether Media, Inc.

No part of this publication may be reproduced in whole or in part without written
permission of the publisher. For information regarding permission, write to
Bellwether Media, Inc., Attention: Permissions Department,
6012 Blue Circle Drive, Minnetonka, MN 55343.

Library of Congress Cataloging-in-Publication Data

Names: Downs, Kieran, author.
Title: Nile crocodile vs. hippopotamus / by Kieran Downs.
Description: Minneapolis, MN : Bellwether Media, 2022. | Series: Torque:
   Animal battles | Includes bibliographical references and index. |
   Audience: Ages 7-12 | Audience: Grades 4-6 | Summary: "Amazing
   photography accompanies engaging information about the fighting
   abilities of Nile crocodiles and hippopotamuses. The combination of
   high-interest subject matter and light text is intended for students in
   grades 3 through 7"– Provided by publisher.
Identifiers: LCCN 2021001443 (print) | LCCN 2021001444 (ebook) | ISBN
   9781644875346 (library binding) | ISBN 9781648344961 (paperback) | ISBN
   9781648344428 (ebook)
Subjects: LCSH: Nile crocodile–Juvenile literature. |
   Hippopotamus–Juvenile literature.
Classification: LCC QL666.C925 D69 2022 (print) | LCC QL666.C925 (ebook)
   | DDC 597.98/2–dc23
LC record available at https://lccn.loc.gov/2021001443
LC ebook record available at https://lccn.loc.gov/2021001444

Editor: Rebecca Sabelko   Designer: Josh Brink

Printed in the United States of America, North Mankato, MN.

TABLE OF CONTENTS

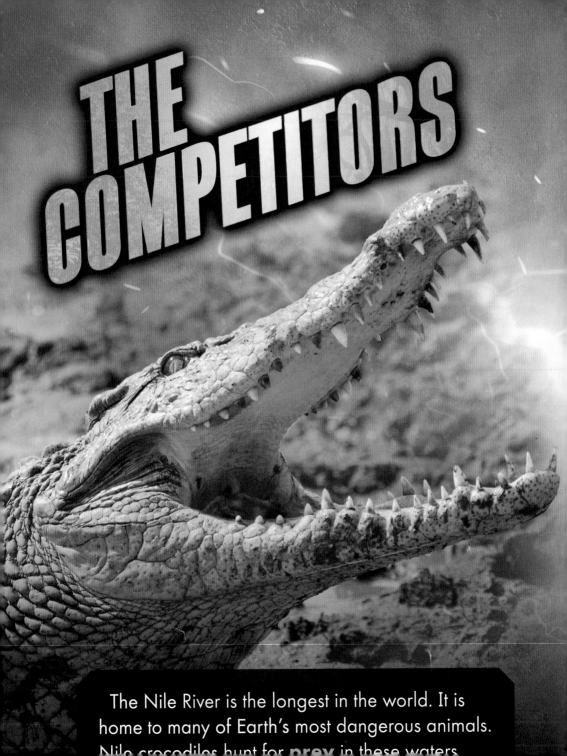

THE COMPETITORS

The Nile River is the longest in the world. It is home to many of Earth's most dangerous animals. Nile crocodiles hunt for **prey** in these waters.

Hippopotamuses are one of the deadliest animals in the world. They also lurk in the Nile's waters. Who would win in a clash between these water beasts?

Nile crocodiles are the largest crocodiles in Africa. They are also the second-largest in the world! They can be up to 20 feet (6.1 meters) long. They weigh up to 1,650 pounds (748 kilograms).

These **reptiles** are found in eastern and **sub-Saharan** Africa. They have dark green or gray scales.

NILE CROCODILE PROFILE

LENGTH
UP TO 20 FEET
(6.1 METERS)

WEIGHT
UP TO 1,650 POUNDS
(748 KILOGRAMS)

| 0 | 5 FEET | 10 FEET | 15 FEET | 20 FEET |

HABITAT

RIVERS   MARSHES   SWAMPS

NILE CROCODILE RANGE

RANGE

7

HIPPOPOTAMUS PROFILE

LENGTH
UP TO 16.5 FEET
(5 METERS)

WEIGHT
UP TO 9,920 POUNDS
(4,500 KILOGRAMS)

0   5 FEET   10 FEET   15 FEET   20 FEET

HABITAT

RIVERS   LAKES   SWAMPS

HIPPOPOTAMUS RANGE

⬜ RANGE

Hippos are **herbivores**. They have brown and gray skin. These large **mammals** can grow up to 16.5 feet (5 meters) long. Their large, round bodies weigh up to 9,920 pounds (4,500 kilograms).

Hippos spend most of their days in water to stay cool. They can be found throughout many parts of sub-Saharan Africa.

RIVER HORSE

Hippopotamus is Greek for "river horse."

9

SECRET WEAPONS

Hippos have powerful bites. Their strong jaws make their mouths dangerous weapons. A hippo's bite can snap a canoe in half!

5,000 POUNDS PER SQUARE INCH

NILE CROCODILE

162 POUNDS PER SQUARE INCH

HUMAN

Nile crocodiles bite with great strength, too. They can chomp through almost anything. Their bites have up to 5,000 pounds per square inch of **force**.

LOOSE TEETH

Crocodiles lose their teeth often. They may go through as many as 8,000 teeth in their lives!

Nile crocodiles have up to 68 cone-shaped teeth. Their razor-sharp teeth easily bite prey. Strong jaws help them hold on.

20 INCHES
(51 CENTIMETERS)

Hippos have large teeth. Their **canine teeth** can be up to 20 inches (51 centimeters) long! The teeth sharpen themselves as hippos **graze**.

STRONG BITES

SHARP TEETH

EYES AND NOSTRILS
ON TOP OF HEAD

Nile crocodiles have eyes and **nostrils** on the tops of their heads. This allows the crocodiles to be **ambush hunters**. They hide underwater while they approach prey. Then they strike!

HIPPOPOTAMUS

STRONG JAWS

LARGE TEETH

CHARGING SPEED

Hippos are able to move quickly on land. They can charge enemies at speeds of up to 30 miles (48 kilometers) per hour. Not much stands in their way!

ATTACK MOVES

Nile crocodiles attack from the water. They snap their powerful jaws around their prey. Their sharp teeth sink into the **flesh**.

Hippos are very **territorial** and will attack anything dangerous. First, they roar with their mouths open wide. If this does not scare enemies away, they are ready to fight!

HIPPO ATTACK!

It is estimated that hippos attack around 500 people in Africa each year.

Nile crocodiles drag their prey underwater. They use their teeth to hold the animal down. The crocodiles will eat all of their prey once it is defeated.

In battle, hippos attack with their canine teeth. They use them to stab enemies. Powerful bites finish enemies off.

READY, FIGHT!

A hippo spots a crocodile approaching. It opens its mouth to scare the crocodile off. But the crocodile springs forward. The hippo readies for a fight.

The crocodile bites the hippo. But the hippo shakes it off. It bites down on the crocodile. One bite is enough. The crocodile is defeated!

GLOSSARY

ambush hunters—animals that sit and wait to catch their prey

canine teeth—long, pointed teeth that are often the sharpest in the mouth

flesh—the soft parts of an animal's body

force—power that has an effect on something

graze—to feed on growing plants

herbivores—animals that eat only plants

mammals—warm-blooded animals that have backbones and feed their young milk

nostrils—the two openings of the nose

prey—animals that are hunted by other animals for food

reptiles—cold-blooded animals that have backbones and lay eggs

sub-Saharan—the area of Africa that is south of the Sahara Desert

territorial—ready to defend a home area

TO LEARN MORE

AT THE LIBRARY

Gagne, Tammy. *Hippopotamuses*. Lake Elmo, Minn.: Focus Readers, 2018.

London, Martha. *Crocodiles*. Minnetonka, Minn.: Kaleidoscope Publishing, 2019.

Schuetz, Kari. *Nile Crocodiles and Egyptian Plovers*. Minneapolis, Minn.: Bellwether Media, 2019.

ON THE WEB

FACTSURFER

Factsurfer.com gives you a safe, fun way to find more information.

1. Go to www.factsurfer.com

2. Enter "Nile crocodile vs. hippopotamus" into the search box and click $\mathcal{Q}$.

3. Select your book cover to see a list of related content.

INDEX

The images in this book are reproduced through the courtesy of: Moncar0, front cover (crocodile); John Carnemolla, front cover (hippo); Jane Rix, pp. 2-3, 20-21, 22-23 (crocodile); Gaston Piccinetti, pp. 2-3, 20-21, 22-23 (hippo); Stu Porter, p. 4; Etienne Outram, pp. 5, 13; diegooscar01, pp. 6-7; Pavel Mikoska, pp. 8-9; Sergey Uryadnikov, pp. 10, 16; Federico Veronesi/ Minden Pictures, p. 11; Lou Coetzer/ Getty, p. 12; JMx Images, p. 14; Roger de la Harpe, p. 14 (sharp teeth); Mari Swanepoel, p. 14 (eyes and nostrils); Gudkov Andrey, p. 14 (strong bite); PhotocechCZ, p. 15 (main, speed); Timothy Craig Lubcke, p. 15 (large teeth); Andrey Bocharov, p. 15 (strong jaws); Leon Vonk, p. 17; AndreAnita, p. 18; Mint Images/ Getty, p. 19.